GAME
FISHING
DEVICES

Game
Fishing
Devices

Douglas C. Townsend

Adam and Charles Black
London

First published 1979
A & C Black (Publishers) Limited
35 Bedford Row, London WC1R 4JH

© Douglas C. Townsend, 1979

ISBN 0 7136 1956 2

Townsend, Douglas C
    Game fishing devices.
    1. Fishing tackle
    I. Title
    688.7'9   SH447

    ISBN 0-7136-1956-2

Printed in Great Britain by
Hollen Street Press Ltd, Slough, Berks.

Contents

Acknowledgement

The Author is grateful to Esmond Drury (Salmon Flies) Ltd. of Spilsby, Lincolnshire, for permission to illustrate their plastic mount and to suggest uses for it. This plastic mount and various spinners, spoons etc. based upon its use, are the subjects of patents or provisional patents held by Esmond Drury (Salmon Flies) Ltd. and must not be reproduced for sale.

Preface

To a dedicated trout and salmon fisherman winters seem very long, as do periods in the fishing season when the water is too high or too low, or when the temperature is too high or too low, or when the sun is too bright or not bright enough, or when the wind is in the wrong direction, or when there are no fish travelling up the river. I spend these periods, or as much of them as I can, in my workshop making tackle. This keeps me in contact with fishing – and surely the next best thing to actually fishing is preparing to *go* fishing?

This little book is intended to describe the things I make and how I make them. Although money can be saved by making fishing tackle, this is not the object of the exercise. It is to enjoy the pleasure which is derived from catching a fish with tackle made by oneself.

Neither is this book intended to deal with the tying of flies or the making of rods, since these subjects and others have been written about so often by authors much more competent in this field. But there are many other things which can be made at home by any reasonably competent handyman with fairly simple tools.

I hope this book will help you to enjoy tackle-making, that you find pleasure in the use of any spare time you can devote to the operation and that, above all, you discover the pleasure of catching fish with home-made tackle.

*To Joan, who suffers
not only from my
fishing activities
but also from the
absent hours I spend
in my workshop.*

1 Making
needle-mounts
for prawns

There are of course many prawn mounts on the market, most of which are designed to make the prawn spin. Why, however, a natural bait like a prawn should be required to spin – which it certainly does not in nature – is difficult to understand. It seems much more appropriate to fish the prawn by the 'sink and draw' method, and the first two mounts are designed for this purpose.

The needle-mount is very simple to make, and provides the easiest and quickest method of mounting a prawn. It does not, however, give protection to the prawn against rocks on the river bottom and, in consequence, one needs a good supply of prawns! Nevertheless, it has the quality of presenting the bait in its natural profile, and light binding with elasticated thread does help to preserve the prawns.

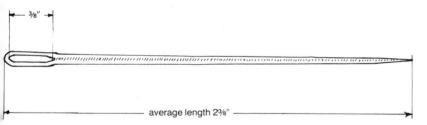

|← 3/8" →|

average length 2⅜"

FIG. 1

In use, the mount should be regarded as a baiting needle. The point is inserted in the head of the prawn and, with the prawn held straight, the nylon trace (about 24″ long with a treble whipped to it) is drawn through the bait and brought out just under the tail. The needle-mount is left on the nylon, and the nylon is attached to the swivel on the end of the reel line with a half blood knot in the usual way. Now reverse the direction of the needle-mount and insert it in the prawn along the line of the nylon, being careful to keep the prawn in a straight line when so doing. You should follow the line of the nylon, which is now running through the prawn. The prawn is held by the needle-mount in a straight line, and the treble will hold it by the head. The treble should be largely concealed by the prawn's whiskers, and in this position it is ideally situated, particularly on those days when salmon tend to pluck at the bait instead of really taking it.

To make a mount, use a 6" (approximate) length of 20 S.W.G. stainless steel wire. The centre $1\frac{1}{2}$" should be reduced in diameter to about half the diameter of the 20 S.W.G. wire; this can be done with a fine file or on a carborundum wheel. This reduced length of the mount must be absolutely smooth since, as you will see, the nylon trace will be in contact with it. A good way of ensuring that the wire is perfectly smooth is to polish it with fine sandpaper.

Resting the wire on an anvil or any other heavy piece of flat metal, beat the wire flat, starting from the centre polished area and working towards the two ends, tapering the wire by beating more at the ends than towards the centre. File the two inner surfaces flat and, using the type of flux specially prepared for soldering stainless steel, tin the two inside flats, but be careful not to allow any solder to get onto the centre 1" which has been carefully smoothed.

Fold the wires so that both sharp ends are together, and solder together. You will now find that although the mount will be tapering in one direction, in the other direction it will be broader at the sharp end than at the 'eye' end. Now file the broader sides down in order to gradually taper the needle in all directions. When this is done, polish with sandpaper and the needle is completed.

The filing of wire is simple enough, but it can be made even simpler by cutting a shallow groove into a piece of hardwood with a tenon-saw. This groove should be approximately half the diameter of the wire in depth; this will be quite sufficient to hold the wire as you file it.

Several of these mounts should be made because they are sometimes lost if a fish is lost and, of course, the rocks on the river bottom will claim a few. Vary them slightly in length to accommodate varying sizes of prawns.

It must be admitted that, if you can find them, long darning-needles will do this job! But usually they rust, and in any case they are not home-made and thus the object of the exercise is completely lost.

2 Making wire-mounts for prawns

This type of mount is perhaps more suitable for use in rocky rivers, since a measure of protection is afforded to the prawn and, as you will see, it is equipped with two hooks.

The mount is made from two lengths of 20 S.W.G. stainless steel wire. The two wires are bent as shown in Fig. 2.

The bending is quite easy if first you make a block of hardwood, and drill and drive into it steel pins at the required centres. The pins should project about ⅛", and the centres are important since if you

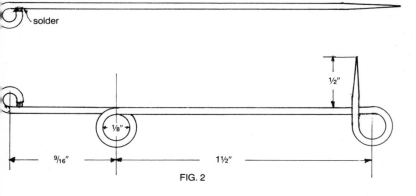

FIG. 2

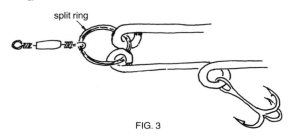

split ring

FIG. 3

make the two hook-holding loops too close together there is a danger that the hooks will interlock and become quite useless. The wire is simply wound round the projecting pins, but a little pincer work is necessary afterwards to ensure neatness. Soldering at the point where shown is a simple operation (but do not forget to use special flux for stainless steel) and it is a precaution against loss.

With the two small loops over one another pass through them a small but strong split ring on which is also included a suitably-sized swivel, as shown in Fig. 3.

Trebles of the size you prefer to use are mounted on each of the two large loops by running them along the wire from the right-hand side as shown in the sketch – firstly into the left-hand loop, and secondly into the right-hand loop. Nip the wires together above the loop with strong pincers to ensure that the trebles remain in the loops. It is possible to replace broken hooks, or to change hook sizes at will – but it is wise to carry pincers in your fishing bag for this purpose.

If you wish your prawns to spin, this can be arranged by making a metal wing and mounting the wires in a rather different way, as shown in Fig. 4.

I have not made a mount like this because I am content that my prawns should *not* spin. Mount the prawns by passing the straight wire through the prawn from the tail, straightening it in the process. Then bring up under the bait that part of the mount holding the hooks. Arrange carefully between the various legs of the prawn (leaving the legs projecting) and press the pointed prong into the prawn's head.

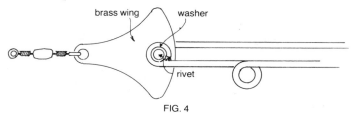

FIG. 4

A light binding with red elasticated thread is all that is required to complete the mounting operation.

Make several of these mounts, so as to have several mounted prawns on hand before you start your day's fishing. It is wise to make them in slightly varying sizes to accommodate prawns of differing lengths, but do not vary the distance between the rings holding the hooks.

3 Making needle-mounts for shrimps

The making of needle-mounts for shrimps is very like the making of those for prawns, except that they are smaller and simpler in manufacture. Start with a short length of 20 S.W.G. stainless steel wire and reduce one end of it to approximately half the original diameter. Polish this end very carefully with sandpaper as described on page 10 because the nylon trace will be in contact with this part of the metal. Fold the reduced wire over as shown on the illustration, solder the end of the reduced length and file down to make a tapered junction. Again clean everything up with sandpaper, sharpen the end away from the eye, and use the mount exactly as described on pages 9 and 10.

The complete mount is shown in Fig. 5.

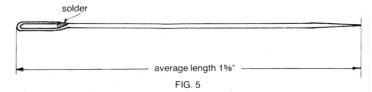

FIG. 5

Make several of these mounts, varying the length slightly to allow for the varying lengths of the shrimps. Test the size of the eye with a piece of the nylon you intend to use when shrimping for salmon. Do not use too fine a nylon, remembering that salmon can be just as heavy caught on a shrimp as on a prawn.

4 Constructing heavy tube flies

You can, of course, buy heavy tube flies, either dressed or requiring dressing, but there is much more satisfaction in making them at home. These tubes are very easy to make and a variety of metal can be used – copper, brass, aluminium etc., depending upon the weight and size of the fly you require.

I make mine from old copper petrol-pipe (obtained from a local garage) which, after carefully cleaning and straightening, is a perfectly suitable material. But it is heavy and it is suggested that the tubes be made also in a lighter material, such as aluminium, to enable varying waters to be fished.

Having obtained the metal and cleaned it, cut the tubes to the various lengths which are required, and then line them with plastic tubing. This tubing is not particularly easy to obtain (it is normally manufactured for surgical purposes), but no doubt a little research will provide a supply.

Having cut the tubes to the lengths required, file the ends flat, then polish both the ends and the tube itself with sandpaper to ensure a polished surface and the filed ends free from rough or sharp edges.

Cut the plastic tube a little longer than the metal tube, insert the plastic into the metal, leaving the plastic projecting as shown in Fig. 6. The plastic tubes should be a fairly tight fit.

Hold a cigarette lighter, match or even a lighted cigarette close to, but not quite touching, the end of the plastic and you will find that it changes shape miraculously, as shown in Fig. 7. This operation is then repeated at the other end and the tube is ready for dressing.

I find the tubes made from copper are far too heavy to use with a fly rod in the normal way, but they are ideal with a light spinning rod. I dress the flies, using various hairs in the usual way, but I do not dress the tubes themselves as I like to use the copper colour as part of the bait. To the tail end of the copper tube I attach a short length of rubber tube, which is a fine receptacle for the eye of a treble. I mount them by threading the trace through the tube, attaching a treble which is held by the rubber tube, and attaching the trace to the swivel of the reel line with a blood knot in the usual way. When made from light metal the tubes can – and should – be cast with a fly rod.

No attempt has been made to suggest the dressing of the tube flies. Dress them according to your own preference.

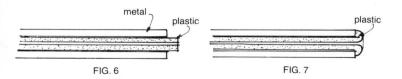

metal ⌐ plastic   plastic

FIG. 6   FIG. 7

5 Making small metal Devons

There are many occasions when a small metal Devon is an extremely good bait, but they are expensive to purchase and often unnecessarily elaborate. They can be made very easily, using the method described on pages 14-15, plus a vein in thin copper as shown in Fig. 8.

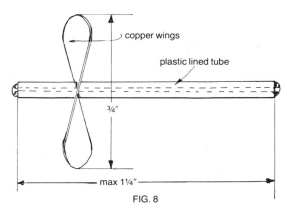

copper wings

plastic lined tube

¾"

max 1¼"

FIG. 8

The copper tube is prepared in exactly the same way as for heavy tube flies, but the length should be restricted to about 1″ or 1¼″. Above this length the commercial type of metal Devons are perhaps preferable.

The metal wings are made in one piece, shaped as illustrated, and drilled to receive the passage of the tube which, after soldering, is twisted to the normal pitch of Devon wings. The operation of soldering should be completed before the tubes are lined, since the plastic will melt with the heat of the soldering.

It is necessary to ensure that the plastic tube has a slightly larger bore than was the case in the tube fly because the Devon must rotate upon the nylon. A small bead should also be included between the Devon and the treble. I prefer to use a whipped-on treble because the pointed end will fit into the bead, holding the hook in a straight line.

The Devons require painting, although if it is intended to use gold as a belly colour, then the copper can simply be polished and lacquered. The rest of the Devon will require painting in colours to suit the water in which you habitually fish. You do not, of course, require a swivel adjacent to the small Devon, but you do need a ball-bearing swivel in the usual position 18″ or so along the trace.

6 Turning wooden Devons

The making of wooden Devons is a rewarding operation, and very worthwhile now that they have become so expensive to buy. You do, however, require a simple lathe for the making of these baits. If you do not possess such equipment, perhaps you can prevail upon someone who has one to allow you to use his workshop.

After much experimenting I find that beech is the best timber to use, although any closely-grained wood, such as walnut, is suitable.

It is proposed to describe the making of 2½″ Devons, but the dimensions given can be scaled up or down to enable a variety of sizes to be made.

Accuracy in cutting the wood is important, and the blanks out of which 2½″ Devons are made should measure 3″ x ⅝″ x ⅝″. Having made these accurately, the most difficult operation is the drilling of the hole down the centre of the blank in the position shown in Fig. 9.

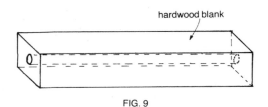

FIG. 9

If the hole position is carefully marked at both ends of the blank it is possible in a lathe to accurately drill from both ends, meeting in the centre with a straight, neat hole. The diameter of the hole will depend upon the metal tube lining you are able to obtain. It should be a tight push-in fit.

Much depends upon the lathe model as to whether or not you need to make a special fitting for the headstock to enable a grip to be obtained on the wood. I found that with my lathe a special fitting was necessary, and I manufactured a tool specially for this purpose, as illustrated in Fig. 10.

Having arrived at this stage in the operation, mount the blank in the lathe and turn the shape of a Devon, leaving (and this is important) short sections of the original square blank in position, as shown in Fig. 11. Thoroughly sand the Devon, as it rotates, until it is absolutely smooth.

Another gadget (Fig. 12), very similar to the joiner's mitre

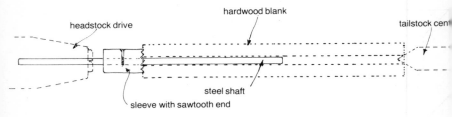

FIG. 10

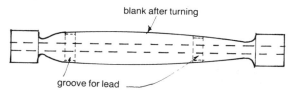

blank after turning

groove for lead

note: ends must be left square

FIG. 11

block, is required for cutting the grooves to receive the wings.

The reason for leaving the square ends in position at this stage is that this enables the almost completed Devon to be held rigidly in the mitre block for the cutting of the first groove with a tenon-saw. If a mark is made in pencil on the mitre block to position accurately the distance of the first cut from the end of the blank, the Devon blank can be rotated through 180°, bringing the end of the block against the pencil mark with the assurance that the second cut will be accurately positioned.

The two square ends can now be cut from the partially completed Devon, the end grain should be cleaned up, and the tube of copper, brass or aluminium pressed into the body of the Devon and cemented into position with Araldite adhesive. Later, when the adhesive is set, the ends of the tube should be filed down neatly to the end of the timber, and the inside of the tube-ends splayed out a little by the use of a counter-sinking bit and a final polish with sandpaper.

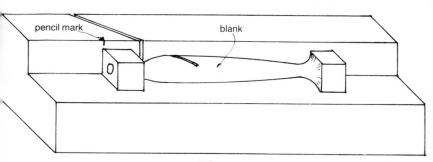

pencil mark

blank

FIG. 12

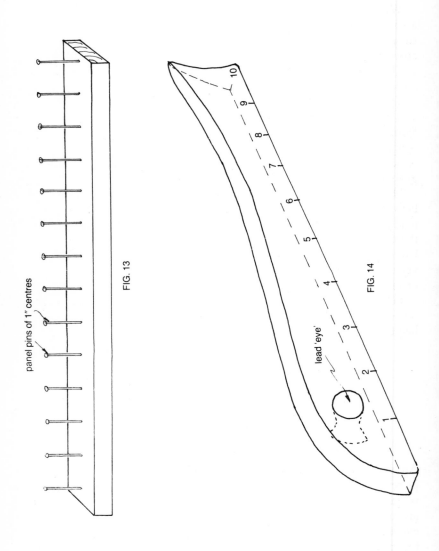

panel pins of 1" centres

FIG. 13

lead 'eye'

FIG. 14

Wings are made from flexible transparent plastic, and I find that
a sample wing made in metal can be used as a template for making
the plastic wings. Place the template on the plastic and scratch a line
around it with a sharp pointed instrument, repeating this operation
until sufficient wings are marked out. Then, with a sharp pair of
scissors, these can be cut out to the exact shape required.

It is possible to make wooden Devons of almost any weight
you require by turning grooves in the body before you take them
from the lathe. These grooves, which vary in size according to the
weight required, are then filled with lead foil or thin lead sheeting,
which is stuck into the grooves with Araldite adhesive. (The
grooves are shown dotted in Fig. 11)

The Devons now require painting. I find them easier to paint
before the wings are placed in position, and although the grooves
tend to fill with paint this can easily be scraped out prior to glueing
them in. The result is a very much more professional appearance.
I find that two coats of shellac as a base coat for the paints helps
very much to maintain its condition when the Devon strikes rocks
or other obstructions.

The painting of Devons is a delicate operation, and a little frame
made for holding them during the drying of the various coats is
helpful. Fig. 13 shows a simple construction.

7 Making
a priest

Anything will serve as a priest – a stone from the river bank, a
piece of driftwood – anything, providing that the fish to be killed
is quickly despatched. Nevertheless, a priest can be a satisfying
instrument, and it is worth going to some trouble to make an
efficient and good-looking one. Fig. 14 illustrates one I have used
for some years.

A piece of really hard wood such as walnut or beech is most suitable. The length may be determined by the size of fish your Association allows you to keep. If the take limit is 10″ then I suggest you make a 10″-long priest, but you should scale this up to make one 12″ or 13″ long for your salmon fishing.

Use a small spoke-shave to shape the wood as shown, leaving the bottom side more or less flat. This can be marked off in inches (or centimetres if you prefer) and you will find it useful for measuring the really big ones!

Be careful when you drill the hole for the eye. First drill the hole, which should be about $\frac{5}{8}$″ diameter, and then slightly bevel it on both sides of the priest like a double dove-tail; this ensures that the lead with which the hole or eye must now be filled will not work loose. To make the lead 'eye', beat a piece of old lead sinker or any scrap lead into a cylinder, and file it down to become a push-fit through the narrow portion of the hole. Make the cylinder slightly longer than the thickness of the priest. Then, gradually, tap the lead into the eye with the domed head of a hammer, working from both sides until the double dove-tail section of the lead is formed. Clean off the surplus lead, apply two or three coats of varnish, and the priest is completed.

8 Constructing
a wading
staff

The wading staff described here is very much more than that – it is also a thumb-stick, a landing-net handle, a gaff handle, a means of weighing your salmon (between 6 and 10 lbs) and a device for carrying your salmon back to the car.

To make the staff you require:—

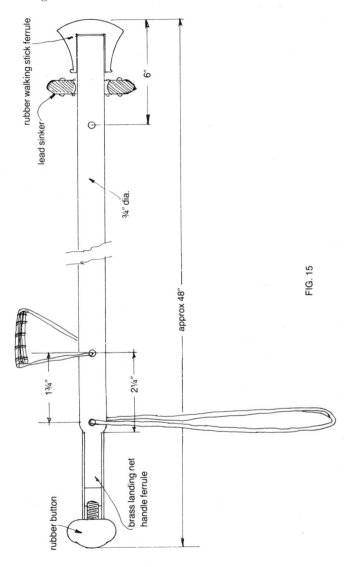

rubber walking stick ferrule

lead sinker

6"

¾" dia.

approx 48"

FIG. 15

1¾"

2¼"

rubber button

brass landing net
handle ferrule

a brass ferrule, as used on a landing-net handle;
a length of hardwood dowelling $\frac{3}{4}''$ diameter and 4′0″ long;
a lead sinker obtainable from any Tackle shop, ($1\frac{3}{4}''$ outside
diameter x $\frac{3}{8}''$ thick);
a rubber ferrule as used on a walking stick;
a pair of strong leather boot-laces;
3 short copper tubes $\frac{7}{8}''$ in length x approximately $\frac{1}{8}''$ bore.

Commence making the staff by ensuring that the length of dowelling
is perfectly straight. Thin down one end of the dowel for a length
of $1\frac{3}{4}''$ until its fits snugly into the brass ferrule and, before per-
manently fixing, coat the wood with Araldite adhesive. Drive the
ferrule onto the timber and leave to set.

Drill three holes to receive the copper tubes in the positions shown
in Fig. 15, ensuring that the holes are drilled accurately through
the centre of the staff. Insert the metal lining tubes and, using a
centre push, splay out the tubes at both ends. When you have
achieved a slight 'funnel' effect at both ends of the tubes file off
surplus metal flush with the timber. Slide the lead sinker onto the
staff, enlarging the hole in the centre if necessary until the sinker
slides along quite easily and, again using Araldite adhesive, cement
the rubber walking stick ferrule onto the end of the staff.

The making of the staff is now virtually completed. All that
remains is to screw the rubber button into the brass ferrule and
thread one of the boot-laces through the first hole from the brass
ferrule end, whipping the two ends together to make a continuous
loop. This loop should be of sufficient length to enable you to
carry the staff over your shoulder. The second boot-lace is threaded
through the second hole, forming a loop about 6″ from the staff.
Double the lace back several times to form a handle, and whip this
handle at intervals with silk, varnishing the whippings when
completed.

The staff now requires calibration to enable you to weigh the
fish. This is done by supporting the handle-loop on a hook and
attaching a weight of 6 lbs onto the long loop. You will now find
that by sliding the lead sinker along the staff it will eventually
balance like a butcher's steelyard. Mark the position of the lead on

the staff. Repeat this operation by adding an additional ½ lb to the loop, and mark the 6½ lbs position. Continue this procedure until the sinker is up against the rubber walking stick ferrule and you will probably find that you have calibrated the staff between 6 and 10 lbs in ½ lb intervals. You can then quite easily estimate where the ¼ lb mark should be if you wish for such fine divisions.

You can also calibrate the opposite side, enabling you to measure a fish up to almost 4' 0" in length (always assuming you are able to catch a fish of this size!) I know that a fish 4' 0" in length will weigh very much more than 10 lbs, but the majority of salmon (at least those *I* catch) do not exceed this weight and when they do I am quite prepared to go to more trouble than merely weighing them with a staff, to find their precise weight.

The numerals you use for calibration can be many and varied, but I purchased a sheet of Letraset Transfer numbers which I found to be quite excellent. Having applied the numbers to the staff, it only requires two or three coats of varnish to perfect what I have found to be an extremely useful implement.

If you unscrew the button from the brass ferrule you can substitute a landing net or gaff if you so wish.

Finally, for carrying your fish home, loop the tail into the leather loop, pass a piece of cord through the copper-lined hole near the base of the staff, and thence through the salmon's gill. You will find that the fish is nicely balanced along the staff, and if you hold the latter in the middle with the salmon draped down below it you can comfortably carry it back to your car. If you wish to weigh fish over 10 lbs you should use a 1" diameter staff and a heavier sinker.

9 Making
a trout balance
and measure

If, like me, you keep a record of all the trout you catch, you will find the instrument described here very useful for measuring and weighing your fish.

The weighing and measuring principle of this balance is very similar to that described on page 25. You require a length of hardwood, (either beech or walnut) about 1' 9" in length and of a section $1\frac{3}{4}$" x $\frac{3}{8}$", a little scrap lead, four square angle cup hooks, a short length of old fishing line and a fairly large fish hook from which you must remove the barb and make the point quite blunt.

Prepare the wood, ensuring that all faces are accurately planed and sanded to as fine a finish as possible. Prepare a piece of lead $\frac{1}{8}$" thick, 2" long x $1\frac{3}{4}$" in width, and carefully prepare a slot at one end of the balance to receive it. Drill a hole 1" from the same end of the balance, slightly bevelling or counter-sinking this at both sides. Prepare and pass through the hole a lead dowel, and hammer it into position along the lines previously described, but not before you have coated the lead and the inside of the groove with Araldite adhesive. Clean off surplus lead and slightly round the corners of the wood.

Drill a small hole at the other end of the balance to receive a cord, pass the cord through the hole and tie a knot to prevent it pulling through. Attach the other end of the cord to the fish hook.

Mark off one side of the balance in inches by shallow saw-cuts. Give a final clean-up with sandpaper and apply Letraset transferable numerals as shown in Fig. 16.

The balance is now virtually completed. All you need to do is to find a convenient kitchen shelf or the base of a high-level cupboard and screw into it 2 cup hooks. Place them in such a way that the balance slides between them as indicated on the sketch. Screw a

Game Fishing Devices

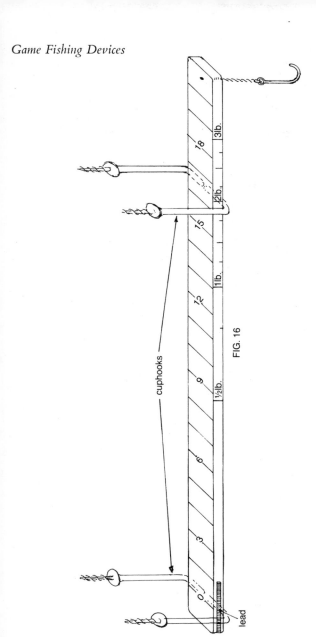

FIG. 16

cuphooks

lead

27

further 2 cup hooks in such a position that they form a rest for the balance when it is not in use.

Now attach a known weight (say $\frac{1}{2}$ lb). Slide the gadget along the cup hooks until it is in balance, and calibrate it on the visible edge to indicate the $\frac{1}{2}$ lb weight. Repeat this operation (in $\frac{1}{4}$ lb stages) up to whatever weight of trout you usually catch. Again make the calibration marks with a saw-cut and apply Letraset numerals. Lastly, apply two or three coats of varnish and the balance is ready for use.

10 *Making stillages for use when whipping rings or ferrules to rods*

The making of these stillages is very simple. All you require is a piece of heavy hardwood approximately 6″ long x 5″ deep x 2″ thick. Carefully clean up the wood to smooth surfaces on all faces, including the end grain. Draw a line round the block to enable you to cut it ultimately into two pieces 6″ x $2\frac{1}{2}$″ x 2″, but before cutting it drill a hole through the centre approximately $1\frac{1}{2}$″ in diameter. Then cut the block and clean up the newly-cut surfaces.

Line the groove on both pieces with felt, and also stick felt on the bottom of both pieces as shown in Fig. 17. The felt in the grooves affords protection to the rod – that on the bottom of the stillage protects your dining-room table! The stillage is used by resting the rod in the two grooves spaced some distance apart on the table. The rod can now be rotated by hand and the whipping silk more easily wound round the rod.

Having made the actual process of whipping somewhat easier, the only problem I have encountered is where the silk starts to climb from the rod over the base of the ring. I find that, if a small triangle of Sellotape is applied, the whipping silk climbs neatly from the rod on to the ring.

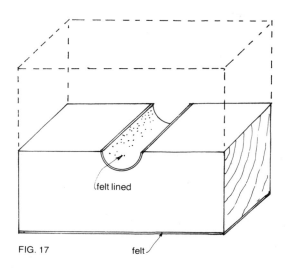

(felt lined

FIG. 17   felt

11 Making a fly head varnishing rack

If you habitually tie your own flies, as I hope you do, you will know how difficult it is to dry the varnish on a fly head. You will also know how easy it is to knock over the little bottle of varnish, and how the needle you use for applying the varnish often sticks to your table.

A frame to overcome these problems is quite easily made from a

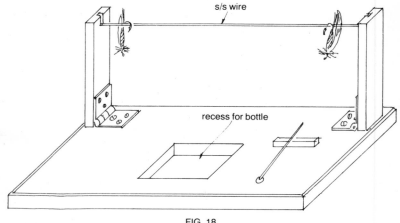

FIG. 18

piece of wood about 9″ x 6″ x ½″ thick, with two small hinged uprights fixed as indicated in Fig. 18, and a piece of stainless steel wire. The bottle is recessed into the base, and a small block of wood is provided upon which the needle can rest when not in use.

12 Making a fly box for pin flies

In the February 1978 issue of *Trout and Salmon* there appeared an article on Pin Flies by Mick Noel-Buxton. It must have inspired many salmon-men to tie some of these easy-to-make flies. No opportunity has yet come my way to try them out in practice but I look forward to testing them in the near future. They are, as

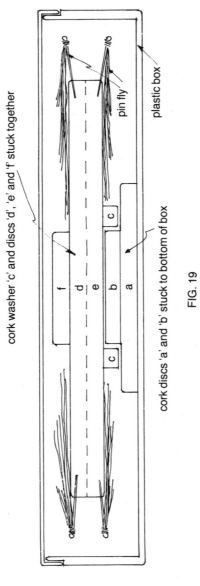

cork washer 'c' and discs 'd', 'e' and 'f' stuck together

plastic box

pin fly

cork discs 'a' and 'b' stuck to bottom of box

FIG. 19

Mr Noel-Buxton says, very easy to tie – this, and the fact that the materials required are inexpensive, tends to make one tie a great number of them. I found that I had tied rather more than fifty in two short sessions, and so the question of a suitable case in which to carry them became urgent and important.

I solved the problem by using a plastic box, which formerly held circular plastic cast holders, and a series of cork discs cut from cork sheeting. A section through the box showing the construction is shown in Fig. 19.

The cork sheeting I used was a sample of cork floor-tiling. I found that although this material was suitable it was rather too hard, and a slightly softer cork would have been better. Any cork into which a pin can be pressed will be suitable.

Cutting the disc is a very simple operation if you have a lathe with a face plate. A wooden disc should be screwed to the face plate; this disc should be slightly larger than any of the discs you require in the making of the fly box. By the simple operation of using tiny panel pins to hold the sheet of cork onto the wood, and holding a strong but sharp knife at the correct position, a disc is produced very quickly. Without a lathe the cork *can* be cut with a strong pair of scissors, but this takes much longer.

Assuming the box to have an internal diameter of 4″ you require the following cork discs:—

a. $1\frac{1}{2}''$ in diameter

b. $\frac{7}{8}''$ in diameter

c. $1\frac{1}{4}''$ in diameter, with a hole in the middle $\frac{3}{4}''$ in diameter

d & e. discs $3\frac{1}{8}''$ in diameter

f. $\frac{3}{4}''$ in diameter

Glue discs a and b together and glue the pair into the bottom of the box, making sure that they are placed centrally. This completes the box itself. The two largest discs (d and e) are then glued together and the disc with the hole (c) is glued to the underside of this thick disc. The final disc (f) is then glued on top. The thickness of this top disc may require increasing or reducing, depending on the depth of the plastic box. When the fly box lid is in position it should almost touch the top, as shown in the drawing. This is to ensure that the removable unit which is to hold the flies does not move about when the case is being carried.

The flies are pressed into the double-thick disc all the way round its circumference (top and bottom of the disc) and it is possible to carry between 80 and 100 flies in this one small case.

The disc dimensions will have to be adjusted if the case you use is not the same as the one described. There is nothing hard and fast about it, but keep in mind the fact that the flies are rather long, and make sure you allow sufficient space for them.

13 Making simple fly line holders

When a fly line is not to be used for a lengthy period it should be removed from the reel, cleaned with the special compound sold with the line, and stored on a fly line holder. These line holders are so very easy to make that one should be provided for each fly line you possess.

All that is required is a supply of ordinary plywood and a length of strong cardboard tubing.

Cut the plywood into pieces of approximately 18″ x 5″. They

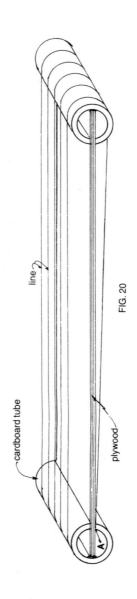

cardboard tube

line

plywood

A

FIG. 20

can be cleaned up with sandpaper and varnished if you so wish. You also require a cardboard tube of approximately 1½″ diameter, which should be cut into 5″ lengths. Run a tenon saw lengthways along the 5″ tubes and press the plywood into the saw cuts, one at each end of the plywood, as shown in Fig. 20.

There is no need to glue the parts together since the spring of the tube is sufficient to hold the three components rigidly in position.

Mount the fly line by inserting the end of the line between the face of the plywood and the cut in the cardboard tube (point A in the drawing) and wind the line from end to end as illustrated. You may prefer to use plastic sheet and tubes for additional strength and permanence, but I have found cardboard and plywood excellent for this purpose and have used holders of this type for years.

14 Tying the 'Andy' knot

Most of us have adapted a standard knot for attaching flies to casts and generally they work well in practice. If they do not we soon change to a knot that does its job without causing problems.

The 'Andy' knot was shown to me by a gillie on the River Tay and I have named this after him. I use it in all cases where the eye of the fly is large enough to take two thicknesses of the nylon cast I happen to be using at the time.

It is really little more than a half blood knot, and differs only in that the cast is passed through the eye of the fly twice, forming a double loop. A perfectly ordinary half blood knot is then formed, and the cast is passed through the loops, which, when pulled tight, trap the nylon by two loops instead of the one usually achieved by

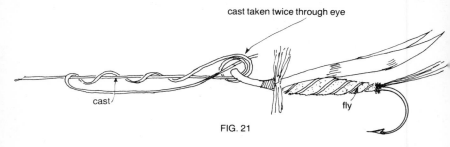

cast taken twice through eye

cast

fly

FIG. 21

the ordinary half blood knot. The eye is more completely filled than it would have been with the ordinary half blood knot, and the fly is held more rigidly in line with the cast.

15 Attaching a cast to a fly line

For years I have endeavoured to find a way of attaching a cast to a fly line so as to produce as small a connection as possible. It is most important, particularly when still water fishing in calm conditions, that a wake is not created at the end of the fly line. The usual methods of attachment involve a loop on the end of a cast and a knot of some kind between the loop and the line. This resulted in there being two knots and one loop to cause disturbance on the surface of the water.

Although it is an admission of incompetence in casting, I have found, on windy days particularly, that far too many of my flies became hooked on to the loop of the cast and formed a tangle that took far too long to free. So I have devised the attachment shown in Fig. 22.

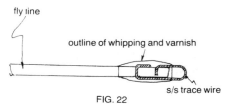

FIG. 22

You will require a short length of 30 lb breaking strain twisted stainless steel trace. Make two holes with a sharp darning needle through the line as shown, thread the trace wire through the holes and shape the stainless steel in accordance with the sketch. Whip over the wire with fine, well-waxed, fly-tying silk, and apply at least three coats of varnish. The distance from the start of the whipping to the end of the wire loop should not exceed $\frac{1}{2}''$.

I have found that the wire trace does require replacement occasionally, but generally I get a full season's fishing before this is necessary. This is just another little job to be done during the close season when you have cleaned the line and mounted it on the fly line holder described on page 33.

16 Sealing
nylon
knots

Generally, when a half blood knot is used (and particularly if you use an 'Andy' knot previously described) it does not slip. But it could, and a fish could be lost, and so any added precaution is worth-while. I found, quite by accident, that if the very end of a nylon cast is touched by the lighted tip of a cigarette, a lighted match or any other form of heat, the nylon melts, forming a little knob rather like a pin head. It occurred to me that this little knob could be quite useful in many cases.

The end of a nylon cast so treated looks as illustrated in Fig. 23A, and it can be used in many ways. Its obvious use is when whipping a hook to nylon as shown in Fig. 23B.

When making tandem flies, for instance, it is most important that the nylon does not become detached from the tail fly, and a knob will add security.

When making nylon mounts for Devons the ends of the four lengths of nylon can be similarly treated if, after bending the nylon around the hooks of the treble, you cut the ends in such a way that no end is immediately opposite another, then form a knob at each end and whip in the usual way. You should never lose a hook or a fish if you follow this simple precaution.

The use of the nylon knob is not confined to the examples suggested above. It can be used when you tie a blood knot or a half blood knot – just leave the ends of the nylon a little longer than you normally do when trimming them off, and then apply the heat treatment. It can be used when attaching the cast to the line with the attachment described on page 36, and when attaching flies to the cast. A particularly good use is when you form a dropper on your casts with a blood knot; the non-dropper should be treated in this way.

Practise this 'heat treatment' with a spare length of nylon, and be very careful not to use too much heat. If you do, the nylon

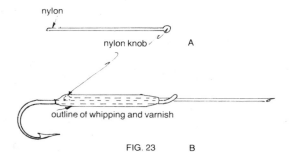

FIG. 23

may ignite and a flame run along the material. A quick touch is all that is required and practice will enable you to make the knob quickly and safely.

17 *Making a frame to aid whipping hooks to nylon*

It is difficult to whip a hook to nylon because of the flexible nature of the nylon and the rigidity of the hook. If, however, the hook and the nylon can be held firmly in line with one another there is no problem.

A frame capable of holding the hook in position and supporting the nylon is called for and the simple structure shown in Fig 24 does help in this operation.

A base board made in hardwood is required, and should measure about 10″ x 3″ and be ¾″ thick. These sizes can be varied a little to allow for the use of any piece of hardwood available. Also required are two hardwood columns ½″ x ½″ x 3″; these columns are let into the base and glued into position. They can also be screwed from the underside of the base as an added security measure.

A fine saw cut is made in one of the columns, and a small cup-hook is screwed into the other as shown in the sketch.

A rubber washer is now required to act as a line grip, and a metal washer above the rubber (screwing it to the base) will secure the nylon during the whipping operations. This line grip could equally well be screwed to the column below the saw cut if preferred.

Place a small rubber band over the cup-hook and round the hook. This rubber band, with the nylon held in the line grip, will provide sufficient tension to hold hook and nylon in line. Whipping

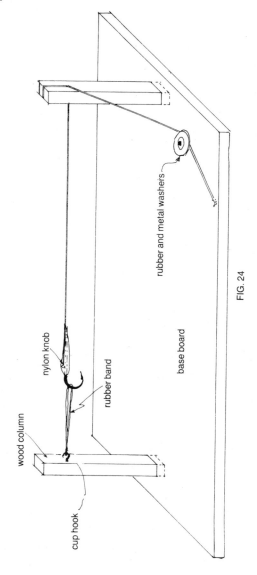

nylon knob

wood column

cup hook

rubber band

rubber and metal washers

base board

FIG. 24

proceeds in the usual way, not forgetting the nylon knob as described on page 37. When you wish to whip a treble to nylon,
proceed as above but use three small rubber bands, one over each
hook, instead of the single rubber band illustrated. By this means the
treble will be held in alignment with the nylon.

This procedure is much the same when making nylon or wire
mounts for Devons. You will, of course, use three rubber bands
to hold the treble in position and a short length of line through
the swivel of the mount, which is held in the line grip as before.
Adjust the length of this line accurately to ensure that the resulting
mount will be the correct length for the Devon.

18 Making a variable weight spinner

Messrs. Esmond Drury (Salmon Flies) Limited produce a red plastic
mount for use instead of the traditional wire or nylon mounts for
Devons etc. The tubes are 3″ long, and have a tulip head to receive
the eye of the hook. The method of using these mounts will be
familiar to you, either from practice or from seeing them described
in the angling press.

These plastic mounts open up a whole new field of possible
development of salmon baits and, of the several I have designed
experimentally, the one shown in Fig. 25 seems to offer some hope
of success.

To make the spinner, use a 3″ Esmond Drury mount. Enlarge the
holes through torpedo-shaped lead sinkers of varying sizes until
they fit snugly on to the plastic mount. The drilling of lead sinkers is
not very easy unless a slow-speed drill is used, but as an alternative

the holes can be enlarged by scraping. The sinkers should be coloured in a variety of colours, black, gold, brown etc.

The only difficult part is the vane unit. You will require a brass tube, the internal diameter of which is a little larger than the external diameter of the Esmond Drury mount. Cut the tube into $\frac{5}{16}''$ lengths. Polish up the cut ends as previously suggested. Cut lengths of strong copper wire $\frac{5}{8}''$ in length, and bend into semi-circles. The wire will be eventually soldered to the tube, but not until you have made the vanes.

The vanes are made out of thin sheet metal – stainless steel, brass, copper, any of these will do, but if you make some from all these metals you will be able to offer your salmon a choice. The shape of the vanes is shown in Fig. 25A. Some should be $1\frac{1}{4}''$ over-all length, and some a little larger, say $1\frac{1}{2}''$. Drill a hole in each with a $\frac{3}{32}''$ drill, and with the round end of an engineer's hammer slightly dish the vane into a shallow saucer shape.

Pass one of the semi-circular wires through the hole in the vane, and solder both ends of the wire on to the tube as illustrated. Polish the vanes with fine glasspaper, and the vane units are completed.

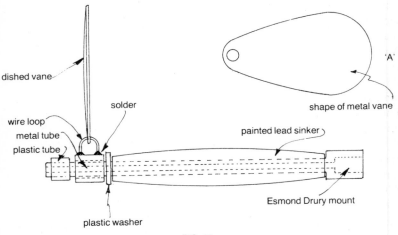

FIG. 25

You will require a small plastic washer to use between the coloured lead sinkers and the vane units, and a length of plastic tube at the front to prevent the vane unit sliding up the line. I find the inner lining of plastic-covered electric cable produces just the right diameter tubing for this purpose. Assembly is shown on the sketch.

19 *Making an experimental spinner*

The plastic mounts supplied by Messrs. Esmond Drury can be used in all kinds of experimental spinners, one of which is illustrated in Fig. 26.

This spinner is based upon the use of spherical lead sinkers. Enlarge the hole in sinkers of varying sizes along the lines described on page 41, and colour them black, gold, brown etc.

A propeller unit is required. This can be made of brass or stainless steel. These units are easy to make if you obtain a strip of metal $\frac{3}{8}''$ wide and cut off $1\frac{1}{2}''$ lengths. Drill a hole in the centre, $\frac{1}{8}''$ in diameter, round off the two ends and twist into a propeller shape.

The body of the spinner is the plastic mount, which, in the case of this experiment, is covered with the outer conductor used in T.V. aerial cable. This I found excellent for the purpose – the bright copper wires seem to be just right with the red plastic of the mount showing through them.

Whip the end of the copper covering just behind the position of the lead sinker; this secures the copper and acts as a stop for the sinker. At the tulip end of the mount arrange a light covering of feather fibres or hairs, much as you would in the making of a tube

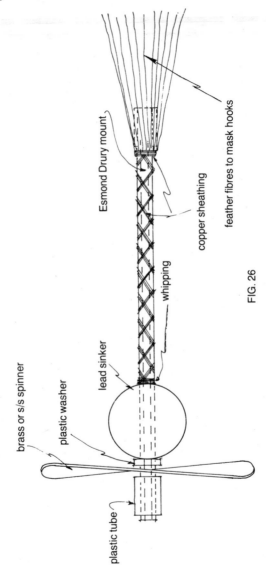

brass or s/s spinner

plastic washer

plastic tube

lead sinker

Esmond Drury mount

whipping

copper sheathing

feather fibres to mask hooks

FIG. 26

fly. The treble will be veiled by these fibres, and the fibres themselves will give some movement in use. Finally, you will need a small plastic washer between the lead sinker and the propeller, and a length of plastic tube at the front to prevent the propeller sliding up the line.

The propeller is the only moving part of the bait, apart, of course, from the movement caused by the hair fibres, which should be sufficiently attractive to interest the salmon.

In use, you simply pass your line through the mount, attach a treble, and draw the eye into the tulip end. If you have made sinkers of various sizes and colours you can ring the changes as you wish to suit the water being fished. You can also, if you have made more than one propeller, change from brass to stainless steel, whichever seems more likely to appeal to the fish (or the fisherman!)

I hope this experimental bait produces a few salmon for you – in any case it is an alternative to the more usual baits, and in my experience there is always the odd daft salmon about!

> '. . . the rod and line,
> True symbol of hope's foolishness, whose strong
> And unreproved enchantment led us on.'

As Wordsworth knew, and as every dedicated fisherman learns, fishing is not just relaxation, the sense of 'getting away from it all', the excitement of playing a fish or even the satisfaction of landing it. It is that feeling of 'hope', whether foolish or not, and the desire to try something new next year, whether on the river or in the workshop.

Tight lines!